Norway Coloring Book

by
Kirsten Sevig

Published by
Skandisk, Inc.
Bloomington, Minnesota

Fourth Printing 2012

Gamle Stavanger is a charming old part of town with
cobblestone streets and well-preserved white wooden houses.

Jon Olav is thinking deep thoughts
as he overlooks the **Geiranger Fjord**.

Fishing is a huge industry in Norway. **Sild** (herring), **makrell** (mackrel), **torsk** (cod), and **flyndre** (sole), pictured from top to bottom, are some of the favorites.

Bryggen in **Bergen** was built by German merchants in the 13th century. It now houses museums, restaurants, shops, and galleries.

This is Sven and his son, Per. Viking boys used play weapons to prepare for battle. Vikings were merchants, farmers, explorers, and warriors.

Helga the Viking runs the farm and the house. As she spins wool into yarn, she teaches her daughter, Liv, to embroider.

The Viking God **Thor** carried a stone hammer that he called *Mjollnir*.
Vikings wore tiny versions of the hammer as good luck charms.

The Baldishol Tapestry from Nes in Hedemark shows a knight with his lance and shield. It was woven in the 13th century using brightly colored yarn.

Trygve is sailing his Viking ship.

Borgund Stave Church in Lœrdal in Sogn was built around 1150. Stave churches featured detailed wood-carvings such as those found on the next two pages. First is a carving of Sigurd the Dragon Slayer from Hylestad Stave Church; second is a hand-carved portal from Urnes Stave Church in Sogn.

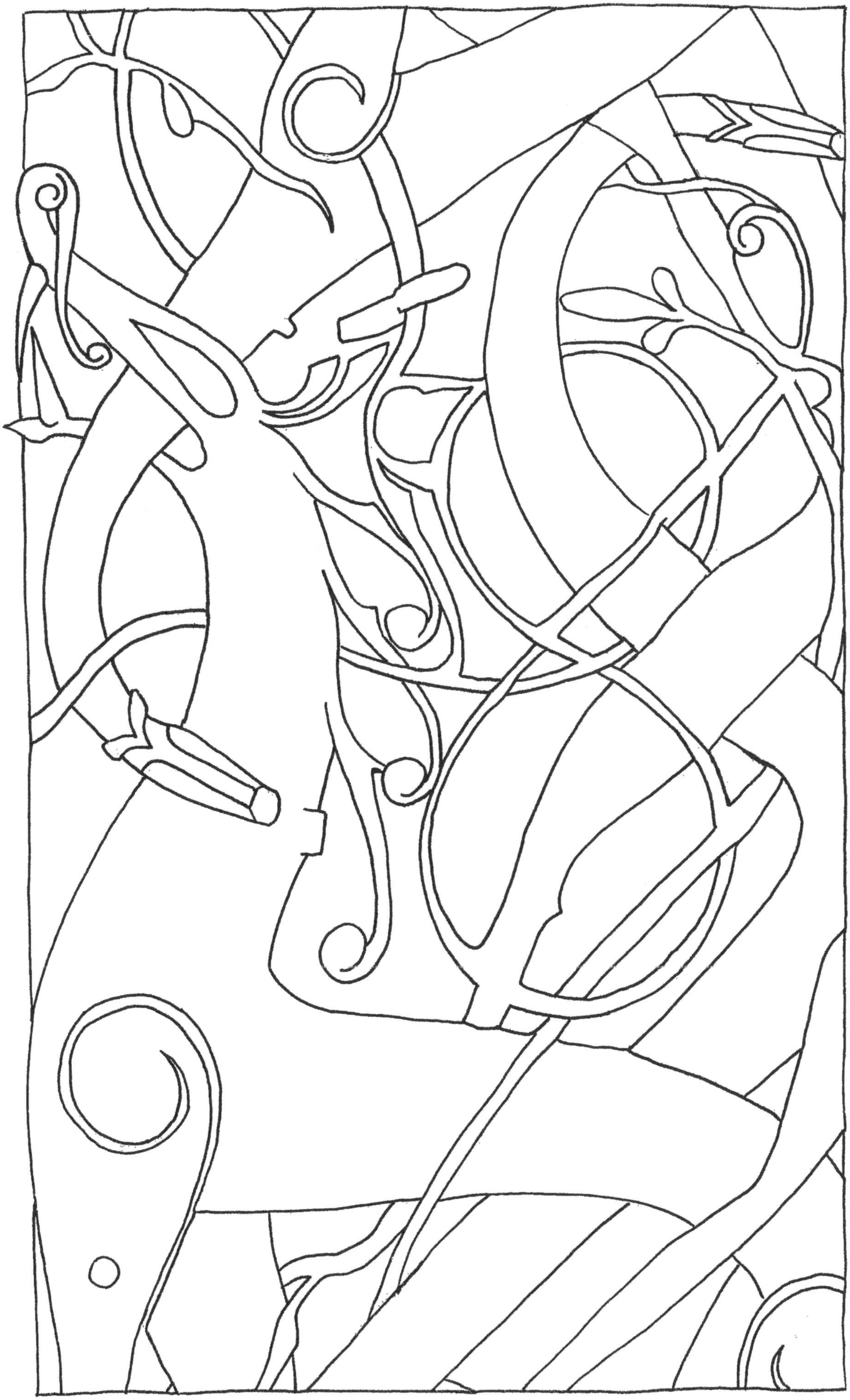

Fastelavnsboller
(Shrovetide Buns)

The four days before Lent are known as Shrovetide, and traditionally that is when these rich buns are eaten—as a last indulgence before Lent. They can be eaten plain, or filled with whipped cream. **Makes 24 buns**

1 pkg. dry yeast
¼ cup warm water
1 Tbsp. sugar
2 cups warm milk
1 egg
½ cup (1 stick) softened butter
1 tsp. ground cardamom
½ cup sugar - add with flour
4 cups flour
1 small beaten egg for brushing

Preheat oven to 375°.
Combine dry yeast, sugar and warm water in bowl. Let it sit for about 5 minutes.

In a separate bowl, beat egg with a whisk. Add warm milk and cardamom. Add the yeast mixture and softened butter. Add sugar and enough flour to make the dough smooth and not sticky. The dough should be soft. Save some flour for rolling out the dough.

Place the dough in a floured bowl and sprinkle flour on top. Cover with a plate or plastic wrap. Place in a warm location and allow the dough to rise until it has doubled in size (about 30 to 45 minutes).

Turn dough out onto a lightly floured board or counter. Divide the dough into 24 pieces (divide into quarters, divide each quarter into 3 pieces, and divide those in half again and you have 24). Form the pieces into round buns and place on a cookie sheet to rise. When they have risen to almost double size, brush them carefully with the beaten egg.

Bake them on the lowest shelf of the oven for 10 minutes. Then move them up and bake until the top is golden brown. Remove from the oven and cool on a wire rack.

Cream filling: Whip 1/2 pint of whipping cream (heavy cream). When almost stiff, add 2 tablespoons of powdered sugar and beat a little longer. When buns are cool, cut them in half (like a bagel). Place a generous spoonful of cream on the bottom half and put the top half back on. Sprinkle powdered sugar on top and serve. Delicious!

Fastelavnsris
(Shrovetide Branches)

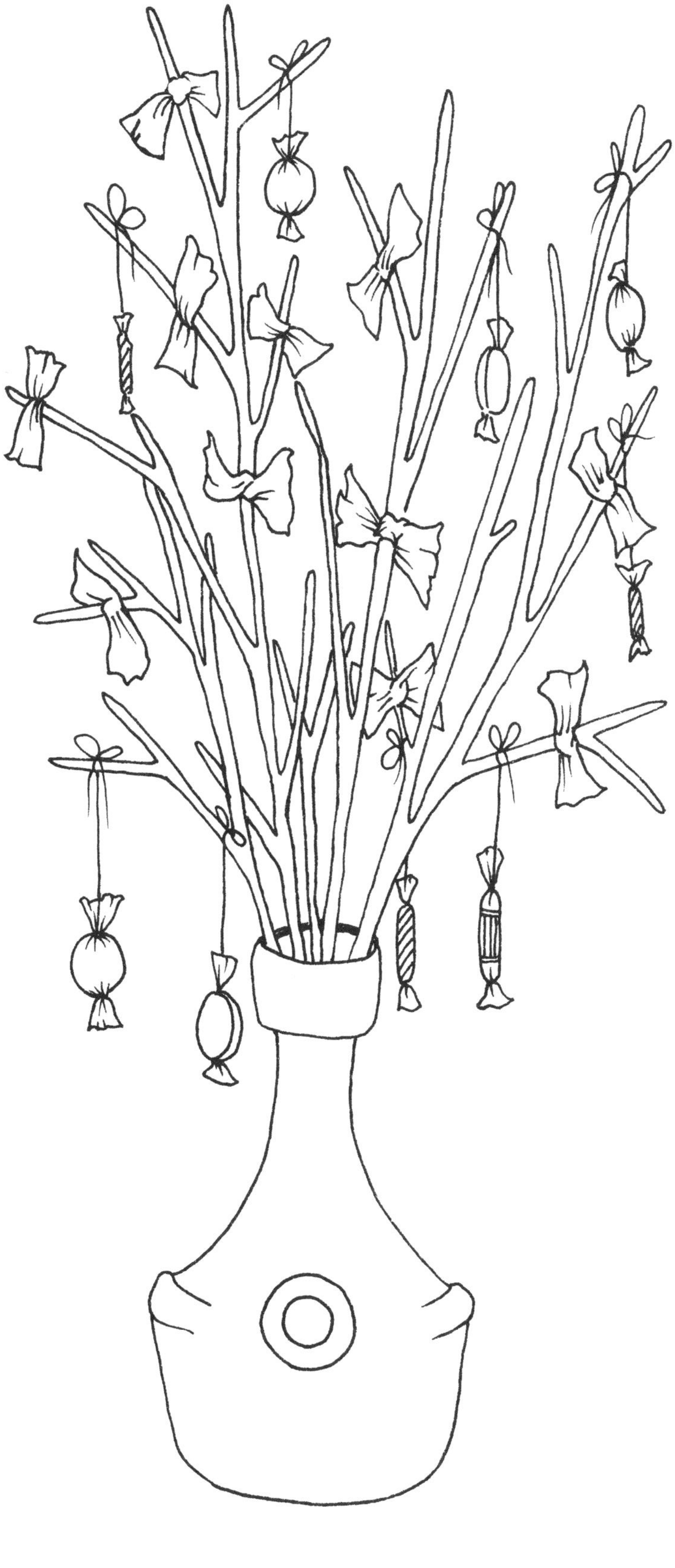

In Norway, *Fastelavn* (Shrovetide Sunday), the last Sunday before Lent, is celebrated with *Fastelavnsboller* and *Fastelavnsris* (Shrovetide Branches).

Children especially enjoy helping to decorate the branches for this colorful display.

To make your own *Fastelavnsris*, you will need to cut branches from trees or bushes (lilacs or birch branches work well). Hold the branches in a cardboard box and spray them with gold spraypaint. Do this outside with the help of an adult. When the branches are dry, place them in a vase with water.

Cut up tissue paper in a variety of colors, making rectangles about 3 by 6 inches. Twist the tissue paper around the branches so they will stay (wrap around once, then give two twists). It will look like you are decorating with little bows!

Then, using ribbon, hang candy from the branches. Make it colorful and fun (caramels, hard candy, and so on). The candy is eaten on *Fastelavn* Sunday, but don't throw the branches away yet for they may start sprouting green leaves!

Ja, vi elsker

Norway's National Anthem

Text: Bjørnstjerne Bjørnson
Tune: Rikard Nordraak

JA, VI ELSKER DETTE LANDET

Ja, vi elsker dette landet,
som det stiger frem
furet værbitt over vannet
med de tusen hjem,
elsker, elsker det og tenker
på vår far og mor
og den saganatt som senker,
drømme på vår jord,
og den saganatt som senker,
senker drømme på vår jord.

YES, WE LOVE THIS LAND OF OURS

Yes, we love this land of ours,
as with mountain domes
stormlashed o'er the sea it towers
with the thousand homes.
Love it dearly, ever thinking
of our fathers' strife
and the land of Saga sinking
dreams upon our life,
and the land of Saga sinking
sinking dreams upon our life.

Syttende Mai: On May 17th, Norwegians celebrate their Constitution Day. Janne and her friends, dressed in their *bunads*, are waving their flags in a big parade.

The Norwegian flag has a blue cross
with a white outline on a red background.

Bløtkake for 17. Mai

(Cream Cake for 17th of May or for Birthdays, etc.)

Bløtkake is one of the most popular desserts in Norway. It is served on just about every special occasion. This recipe is especially made for *Syttende Mai* (the 17th of May, a national holiday), since the cake is decorated to look like the Norwegian flag!

Preheat oven to 350°. Prepare a rectangular (9" x 13") cake pan by lining the bottom of the pan with a piece of parchment paper. Secure the paper to the pan with a small dab of butter in each corner.

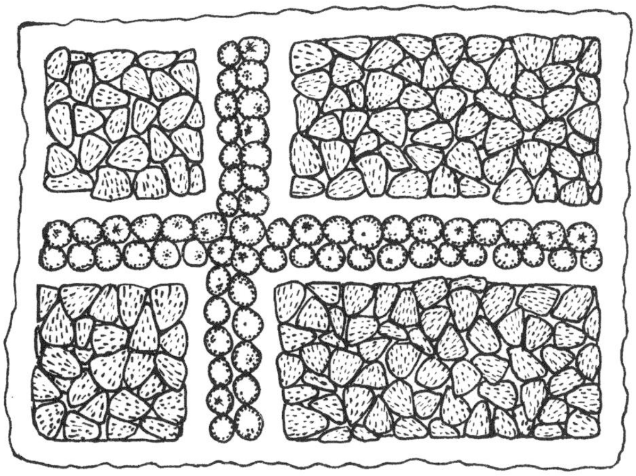

Ingredients:

Cake:
- 8 large eggs
- 1 cup sugar
- 1¼ cup flour (sifted)

Filling:
- 2 cups fresh or frozen raspeberries or cut-up strawberries
- 1½ pints whipping cream
- 3 Tbsp. powdered sugar

Decorations:
- Strawberries (cut in half) or raspberries for the four red portions
- Blue grapes (cut in half), or blueberries for the cross in the middle

Beat eggs and sugar until stiff (about 10 minutes). Gradually fold in the sifted flour, mixing by hand. (Do not stir more than necessary.) Pour mixture into prepared pan.

Bake at 350° for about 30 minutes. Turn oven off. Open oven door and let cake sit for 2 minutes before taking it out. Let cake cool. Cut around the edges of the cake pan with a knife, and loosen the cake. Turn pan upside down on a cooling rack so cake comes out of pan! Let it cool completely. If cake is too big you can divide it in half and freeze half in a one gallon freezer bag for future use. Your cake will then be a smaller flag.

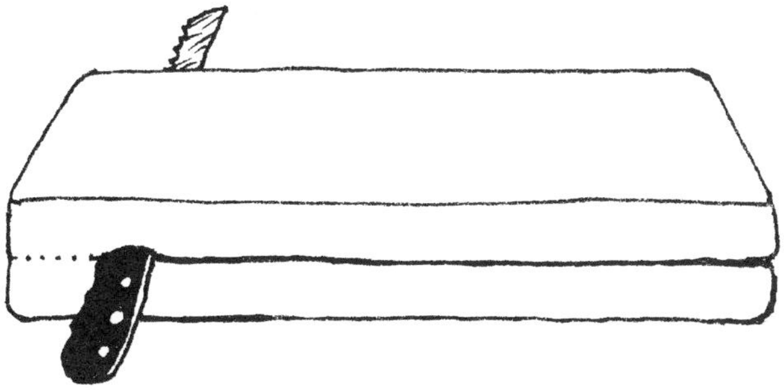

Have an adult help you cut the cake in half horizontally using a knife in a sawing motion. Place the bottom layer on a serving platter. Spread a layer of fruit (raspeberries or cut-up strawberries) on top.

Whip the cream. When it is fairly stiff, add powdered sugar and beat until stiff. Spread 1/3 of the cream on top of the berries. Place the other layer of cake on top. Spread the rest of the cream on the top and sides of the cake. Decorate the top of the cake to look like a Norwegian flag (see illustration above). Put the cut side of berries down. Enjoy this delicious Norwegian dessert.

Rosemaling in the **Hallingdal** style.

Rosemaling in the **Telemark** style.

Reidun and Sindre are wearing *bunader* (folk costumes) from **Gudbrandsdal**. Her skirt is blue with yellow and red flowers on it. Her vest is red and her shirt is white. He is wearing a white jacket with red trim, and white socks. His pants are black, and his vest is red and green plaid.

Kristine and Erik are wearing *bunader* (folk costumes) from **Hallingdal**. She is wearing a black dress with colorful embroidery on the top and bottom, and a white shirt. He has a white jacket with red and green embroidery, a red vest, and black pants with colorful emboridery.

Ingrid wishes her father good luck before the Easter reindeer race in **Kautokeino**, in northern Norway. Their Sami folk costumes are colorful and warm.

Martin and Sølvi, dressed in **Setesdal** *bunader*, are performing a traditional walking dance called *gangar*.

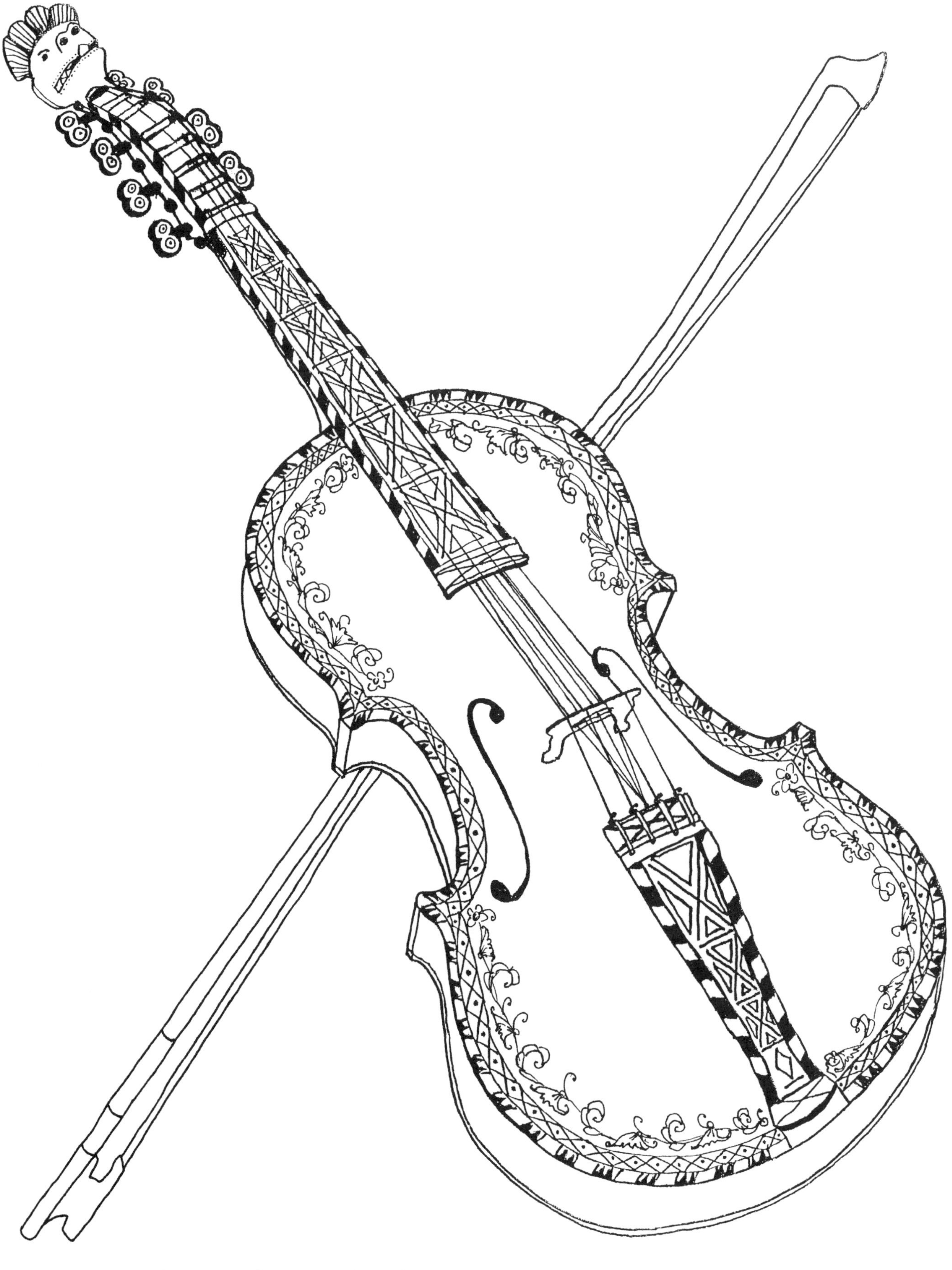

The **Hardanger fiddle** was first made around 1650 in the Hardanger area of Norway. It has an extra set of strings that give it a unique sound. It is a beautifully decorated instrument.

Kirsten, wearing a **Telemark** *bunad*, is leading Mari, the bride, in an old-fashioned Norwegian wedding procession.

Knut, the billy goat, is enjoying fresh grass on the rooftop of the *stabbur*, where food is stored.

Gro has just milked the goats. She will make
geitost (goat cheese) with the milk.

Tilslørede bondepiker

(Fancy Farm Girls)

This is a special summer dessert. If you have lots of apples you can make your own applesauce by cooking peeled apple slices in water until they are soft. It's ok for the sauce to be lumpy. Add sugar until desired sweetness. **Serves six**

1½ cups crushed graham crackers
(Put them in a plastic bag and crush them with a rolling pin or bottle.)
4 cups applesauce
1 quart whipping cream, whipped with 3 Tbsp. powdered sugar

Make layers of graham crackers, applesauce, and cream. Each layer should be about 1/2 inch thick in a glass serving bowl. Decorate with cream on top.

Sigbjørn and Camilla sing by the bonfire in celebration of **St. Hans Eve** (June 23rd).

Edvard Munch (1863-1944) was a famous Norwegian artist.
The Scream is one of his best-known paintings.

Theodor Kittelsen (1857-1914) is well-known in Norway for his paintings of trolls and illustrations of Norwegian fairy tales. This is *Kvitebjørn Kong Valemon* (*White Bear King Valemon*).

Foreldrestolthet (Parental Pride) by Norwegian artist **Theodor Kittelsen**.

Forest trolls may be big and strong, but Norwegians have discovered that they are easy to outwit!

Flettede Julekurver
(Woven Christmas Heart Baskets)

In Norway, woven heart baskets are one of the most common Christmas tree decorations. Traditionally they are made with red and white glossy paper. To make these baskets you will need two sheets of paper in contrasting colors, a ruler, scissors, and glue to attach the handle to the insides of the basket. Often they are filled with small wrapped candies when hung on the tree.

Step 1 -
Take two different colored sheets of paper and lay them on top of each other with the edges even. Fold the paper in half as shown.

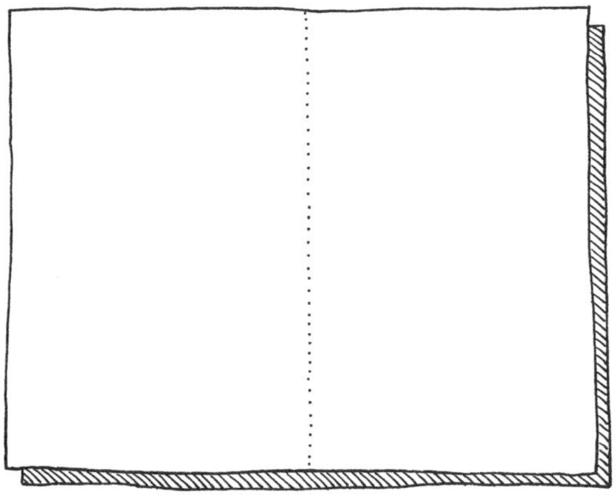

Step 2 -
Cut a 1" strip off of one edge for the handle. Cut the paper as shown. Do not cut the fold!

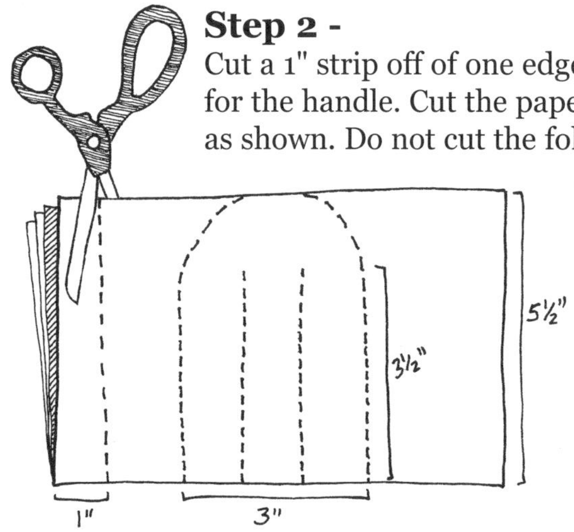

Step 3 -
Arrange the two pieces of paper like this and start to weave, following the illustrations. You may need a grownup to help you.

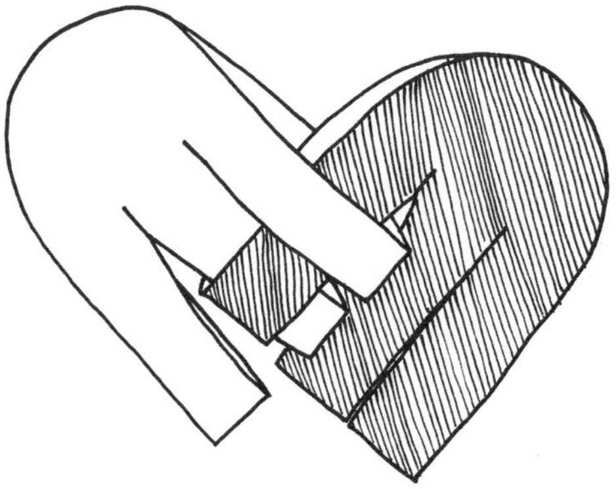

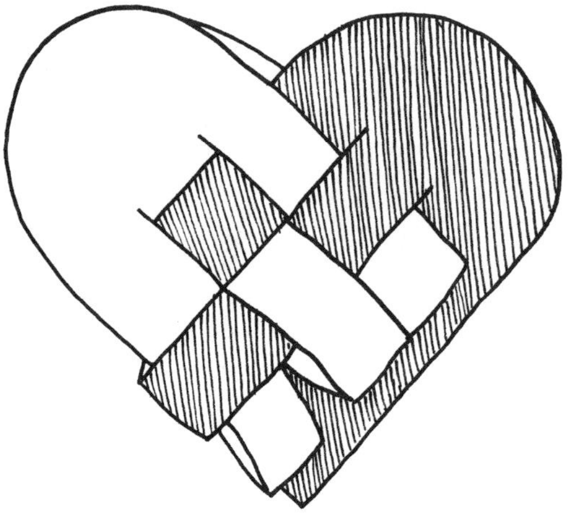

Step 4 -
Glue the handle in place on the inside. Let it dry. Hang it on the tree and fill with candy at Christmas.

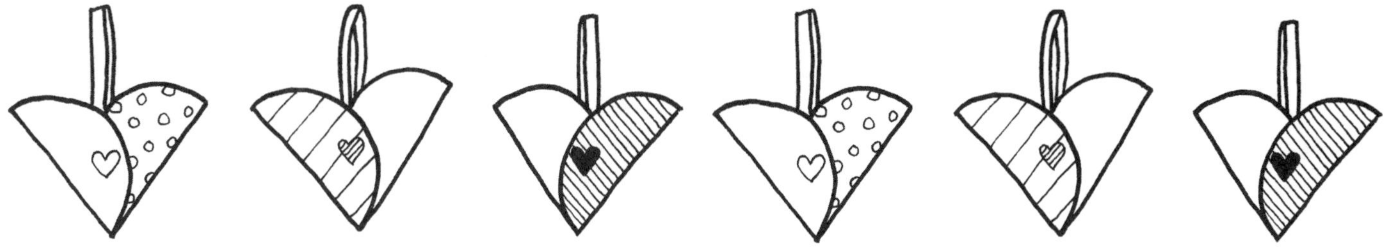

Lette Julekurver *(Easy Christmas Baskets)*

Adventkrans med Potet

(Potato Advent Wreath)

One of the best parts of waiting for Christmas is lighting a candle on the advent wreath every Sunday during Advent. You can make your own advent wreath using potatoes and evergreen branches!

Supplies:

- 2 large baking potatoes
- 4 candles
- aluminum foil
- evergreen branches
- a base on which to place the wreath (a large plate or tray, or cardboard covered with foil)

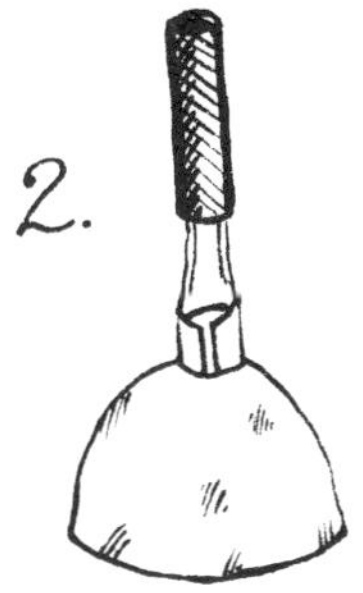

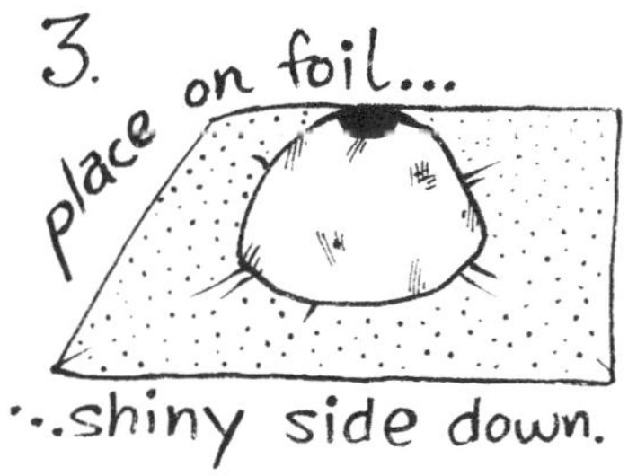

Cut potatoes in half (figure 1). Set them cut side down. Use an apple-corer to cut a hole down through the center of each potato half (figure 2). Remove the center of each potato.

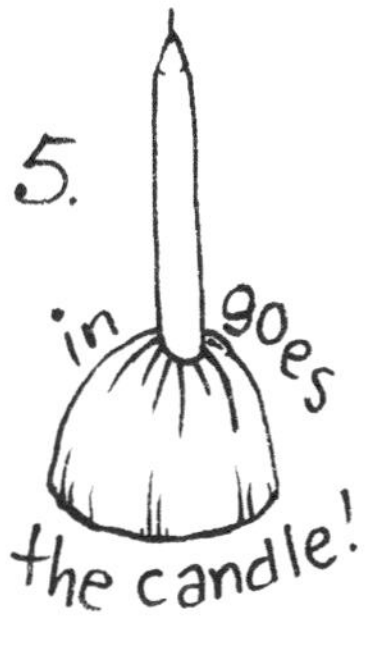

Place each potato half on a piece of foil, shiny side down (figure 3). Bring the edges of the foil up toward the center so it covers the potato (figure 4). Insert a candle in the hole (figure 5). Place the candles on a platter or base as shown, and decorate with small evergreen branches (figure 6).

På låven sitter nissen

Text: Margrethe Munthe
English Text: Mike Sevig
Tune: Traditional

PÅ LÅVEN SITTER NISSEN

1. På låven sitter nissen med sin julegrøt,
   så god og søt, så god og søt.
   Han nikker og han smiler og han er så glad,
   for julegrøten vil han gjerne ha!
   Men rundt omkring står alle de små rotter
   og de skotter, og de skotter.
   De vil også gjerne ha litt julegodter,
   og de danser, danser rundt i ring!

2. Men nissen se han truer med sin store skje,
   "Ja, bare se og kom av sted!
   For julegrøten min den vil jeg ha i fred,
   og ingen, ingen vil jeg dele med."
   Men rottene de hopper og de danser,
   og de svinser, og de svanser,
   og de klorer etter grøten og de danser,
   og de står om nissen tett i ring.

3. Men nissefar han er en liten hissigpropp,
   og med sin kropp, han gjør et hopp:
   "Jeg henter katten hvis der' ikke holder opp.
   Når katten kommer skal det nok bli stopp!"
   Da løper alle rottene så bange,
   ja så bange, ja så bange,
   og de svinser og de svanser noen ganger,
   og en, to, tre, så er de vekk!

THE NISSE* IN THE BARN

1. The nisse in the barn has got his Christmas treat,
   so good and sweet, so good and sweet.
   He nods his head and smiles, oh so happily,
   'cause Christmas pudding he just loves to eat!
   And round him stand the rats that think he's sharing,
   and they're staring, and they're staring.
   They are also very fond of Christmas pudding,
   and they're dancing, dancing in a ring!

2. The nisse starts to threaten with his great big spoon,
   "You better watch out! You better leave soon!
   My Christmas pudding, that I want to eat myself,
   and no one, no one's going to help himself!"
   But the rats are now a-hopping and a-dancing,
   and they're swaying and they're prancing.
   They just want to have some pudding so they're dancing,
   and the nisse's in the middle of their ring.

3. But nisse has a temper when things don't go well,
   so nisse jumps up, and gives a yell:
   "If you don't quit right now, my friend, the cat I'll tell.
   When he comes out, you'd better run, or else!"
   Then the rats, they ran, their eyes were filled with fright,
   filled with fright, filled with fright,
   so they darted to the left and to the right,
   and one, two, three, were out of sight!

This nisse is enjoying his Christmas porridge
while a rat looks on. *A ***nisse*** is a little elf.

Risgrøt *(Rice Porridge)*

In Norway, this traditional pudding is always served in the afternoon on Christmas Eve. Often an almond is hidden in the pudding. The person who finds the almond in his or her bowl receives a treat (usually a marzipan pig)! **Serves four**

1 cup water
¾ cup medium grain rice
1 quart whole milk
½ tsp. salt
1 Tbsp. sugar

Heat oven to 300° then turn it off!
Cook the rice in the water, allowing the rice to simmer under cover until the water has evaporated. Add milk and bring to a boil while stirring. Cover the pot and place it in the warm oven for about 1 1/2 hours.

Return the porridge to the stovetop and reheat while stirring. Add salt and sugar. Stir and serve with a pat of butter on top. Sprinkle with cinnamon and sugar.

Riskrem *(Rice Cream)*

For a special Christmas Day dessert, double the recipe above and use the cold leftover porridge for this delicious treat: **Serves four**

¾ cup whipping cream
2 Tbsp. sugar
1 tsp. pure vanilla extract
a few drops of almond flavoring
2 cups cold rice porridge

Whip cream with sugar, vanilla, and almond flavoring. Mix this into the porridge. Spoon the porridge into individual serving dishes and serve with sweetened raspberries on top (thawed frozen raspberries can be used)!

After the *nisse* has had his fill of Christmas porridge,
he takes care of the animals in the barn.

According to Norwegian legend, the *nisse* is the protector of the farm through many generations. He is very small, has a long beard and wears a red cap. His only demand is a bowl of rice porridge on Christmas Eve. Ah, but if the farmer happens to forget, there will be trouble! Instead of protecting the farm and family, the *nisse* will play tricks on them!

O Jul med din glede

Text: Gustava Kielland
Tune: Traditional

1. O jul med din glede og barnlige lyst,
   vi ønsker deg alle velkommen.
   Vi hilser deg alle med jublende røst,
   titusende ganger velkommen!

Refreng:
   Vi klapper i hendene, vi singer og vi ler,
   så glad er ve, så glad er vi!
   Vi svinger oss i kresten og neier, og bukker.

2. I Østerlands vise, i tre stjernemenn,
   vi vet jo nok hvorhen i drage,
   ti vi ville også så gjerne derhen
   og eder på reisen ledsage.

3. Så rekker jeg deg nå med glede min hånd.
   Kom, skynd deg og gi meg den andre.
   Så knytter vi kjœrlighets hellige bånd
   og lover å elske hverandre.

1. O Christmas with joy & with childlike delight,
   we give you our heartiest welcome.
   our voices we raise in a song clear and bright
   to bid you ten thousand times welcome!

Refrain:
   Our hands we now will clap, we're singing
   and we laugh, so glad are we, so glad are we!
   We swing around a circle and curtsy, and bow.

2. O wise men who came from the land of the East,
   we know of the place you are seeking.
   We pray we may join you in your holy quest,
   and follow the star brightly beaming.

3. In joy and thanksgiving I offer my hand.
   Come, hurry and give me the other,
   that we be united in this sacred band
   and promise to love one another.

Mona reaches up to place a star on top of the Christmas tree, while Lars hangs a heart-shaped basket on a branch. Other decorations include glass balls and candles. Strings of Norwegian flags and tinsel garland hung vertically add to the festive look. The tree is placed in the middle of the room so everyone can dance around it singing the song on the opposite page.

Trolldeig

(Troll Dough)

These ornaments are easy and fun to make out of dough. You'll need to ask an adult to help you get them in and out of the oven.

1 cup flour
1 cup salt
¾ cup water (luke-warm)
1 Tbsp. wallpaper glue
1 Tbsp. oil (olive oil or soya oil is ok)

Mix together all ingredients and knead the dough well (for about 10 to 15 minutes). It should be firm and smooth and easy to work with. If it is too dry, add a little oil or moisten your hands. If it is too soft, add a little flour and salt. Let the dough rest in a tightly-sealed zip-lock bag for at least 30 minutes. (It may be stored in a a zip-lock bag in the refrigerator until you are ready to use it. It will keep for several days.)

Shape the dough by hand or roll it out with a rolling pin. If you wish, cookie cutters can be used to make shapes. If you are making ornaments for hanging, make a hole in the top before baking. You can use a thick straw to make the holes! Make your ornaments on parchment paper, then move the paper with the ornaments on it to a baking sheet.

The oven must be set at a very low temperature to avoid cracking the ornaments. Bake for a total of 4 to 6 hours, increasing the temperature every 1 or 2 hours as follows:

1. 100° 1 - 2 hours
2. 150° 1 hour
3. 175° 1 - 2 hours
4. 200° 1 hour

Baking times are approximate. Drying time varies with size and thickness of ornaments. Check often to see if the ornaments are dry, and to make sure they are not getting burned.

When the ornaments are cool, you can paint them with watercolor or acrylic paint. When the paint is dry, spray them with one or two coats of varnish (cover the area well before you do this). Remember, these ornaments are decorations—do not eat them!

Winter fun in Norway includes cross-country skiing, sledding and tobagganing, and using a *spark* (kicksled) like the one Helene and Magnus are using in this picture.

Norway's National Coat of Arms *(riksvåpen)* dates back to about 1280. The lion is a symbol used by the Norwegian kings. The axe is a symbol of St. Olav. The lion and the crown are golden, the shield is red.

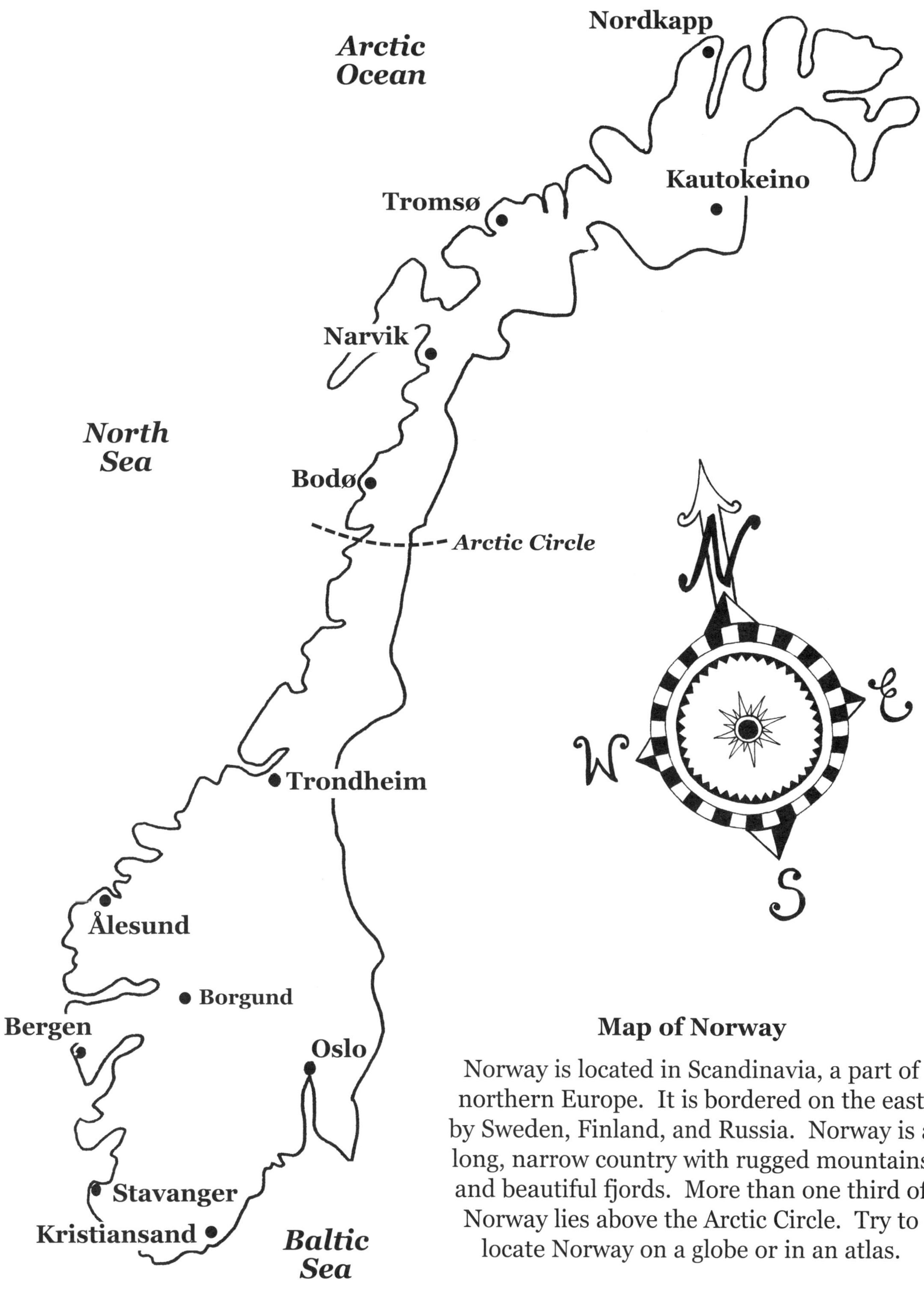

Map of Norway

Norway is located in Scandinavia, a part of northern Europe. It is bordered on the east by Sweden, Finland, and Russia. Norway is a long, narrow country with rugged mountains and beautiful fjords. More than one third of Norway lies above the Arctic Circle. Try to locate Norway on a globe or in an atlas.

Tynne Pannekaker *(Thin Pancakes)*

There's nothing like pancakes to get you going on a cold winter morning:

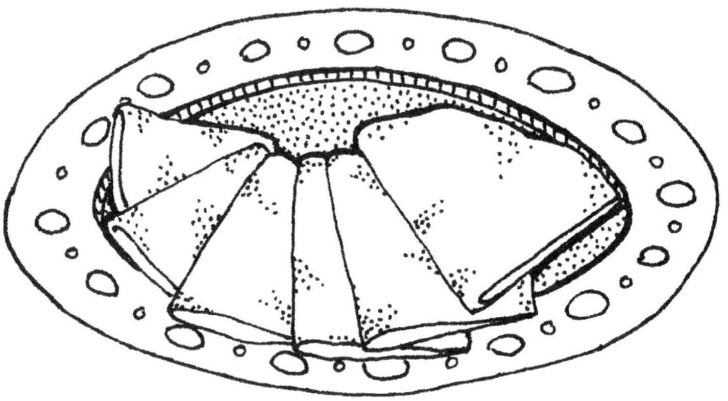

Ingredients:

- **3 cups milk**
- **½ tsp. salt**
- **1 Tbsp. sugar**
- **2 cups flour**
- **2 eggs**

Beat together all ingredients with whisk. Do not overbeat. If the batter is too thick, add a little milk; if too thin, add a little flour. Let sit 10 to 15 minutes before frying pancakes. Unfold a pancake, spread with blueberry jam, roll it up and enjoy!

Serves four

Snøball Lykt *(Snowball Lantern)*

Lighten up a winter evening with these glowing snowball lanterns.

Make 25 firm snowballs the size of baseballs. Place 9 snowballs in a circle, just touching each other. Place a candle in the middle of the circle. You can use a fat candle that stands up by itself, or a short candlestick in a pot (or other kind of holder). Make a snowball pyramid with 7 snowballs in a circle on top of the first 9 snowballs. Use 5 snowballs in the third level, and 3 in the last. Save 1 snowball for the top.

Carefully light the candle with a long-handled match (or grill lighter) through one of the holes on the side of the pyramid. The light of the candle will shine through the holes. Don't put the last snowball on top of the pyramid until you want to snuff out the candle. It will melt and drip down on the candle.

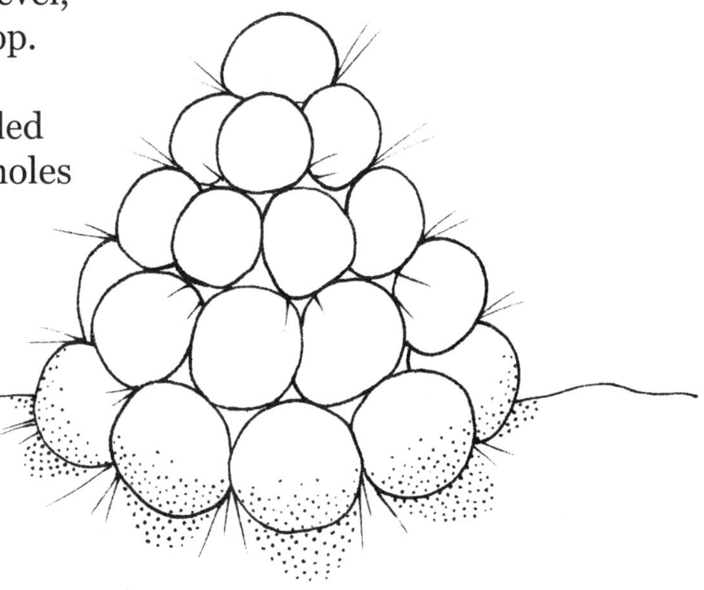